# Earthly
# **Poems by Jean Follain**

Selected and translated by Andrew Seguin

The Song Cave

The Song Cave
www.the-song-cave.com

Cover image: "The Gust of Wind," by Camille Corot, 1871.

Design and layout by Janet Evans-Scanlon



ISBN: 979-8-9912988-5-8
Library of Congress Cataloguing-in-Publication Data has been applied for.

FIRST PRINTING

# Contents

***1957*, prose poems from *Tout Instant***



***1960 – 1971***

# Introduction

Jean Follain was struck by a car and killed just after midnight near the Place de la Concorde in Paris in 1971, a brutal irony considering how many of his poems are rutted by farm carts and horse carriages and apple wagons. Born in 1903 in Canisy, a small town in Normandy, Follain watched the men and animal-powered conveyances of his rural childhood go off to the First World War, most never to return. The embers of that agrarian world were later extinguished by increasing industrialization and the Second World War. "There are almost no more horses," Follain wrote in 1960.

Follain's poems emerge from that remembered landscape of farmers, wheelwrights, seamstresses, animals and fields, but to call them pastoral would be a misdirection. They have more in common with the quantum world, where matter is simultaneous, both particle and wave. Follain will find the eternal in a kernel of wheat, tumbled into the fold of a dress, or a tool left out in a garden. For time is his ultimate subject—how it overlaps and doubles back in memory, how each arriving instant contains past and future, and how sad it is to lose it.

> the boy has such bright eyes
> then there's the girl who will die young
> and one whose body will be alone
> they are all washing their hands in shadow

beside lush vegetation
and are still in that time
of living in eternity.

("The Children," from *Territoires*, 1953)

The poem occurs in present tense yet the children's future is present, too, being seen by someone who knows what is coming, and is therefore looking back. It is this simultaneity of remarkable things, terrible things—thus ordinary things—that Follain is always finding words for, and which gives his poems their particular pangs and mysteries.

He sounds like no one else. His phrasing, his syntax, his curious punctuation, seem to take the mind out like a dog, let it sniff a post, before arriving somewhere unexpected. Some of this is just how the French language works, but much is Follain's peculiar sense of joinery—who put this thing together this way? Where are the nails?

As many have remarked, Follain almost never writes from "I." He sets out more frequently from "*on*," the third person pronoun in French that in English can be rendered most literally as "one," or, in other contexts, "you" or "they" or "we." It can also suggest the passive voice. Follain's third person evokes an impassive and seemingly omniscient gaze, located at a remove, surveying the landscape and its species, yet intimate with the most minute particulars. A specific consciousness, with intense affection for the world around it, is clearly present, but it is less interested in itself than in tracing the connections suffusing all things, the umbels of plants, an insect crawling up a boot, the woman sitting on a hearth asking "why beings and things / and not nothing."

A timeless question. And Follain's poems do feel timely, as the ravages of our human-centric worldview upon plants and animals—our species forgetting that it, too, is an animal among them—mount toward irreversibility, as war unfolds where it has so many times before.

After his Norman upbringing, Follain studied law and became a lawyer in Paris. His poems began to appear in journals alongside some of the Sagesse group, and the first of his thirteen books of poems, *La Main chaude*, was published in 1933. Prose works soon followed, including, in 1935, *Paris*, a beautiful *flânerie* of the city he made his home, and several memoirs of his childhood in Canisy and the nearby city of Saint-Lô, which was decimated by Allied bombs in WWII. Follain later became a magistrate in Charleville (the natal village of Rimbaud), to which he commuted while still living in Paris on the Place des Vosges.

Follain traveled widely throughout the 1960s, to Peru, Chile and Bolivia, to Côte d'Ivoire and Senegal, but these voyages barely surface in the later poems. His cosmopolitanism and catholic interests come forth more in his diverse prose. He wrote a celebration of the potato, which included a memory of the particular *tangue*, or mud, that was harvested in the Norman estuaries and used to cultivate a varietal called Early Rose, grown by his father; a glossary of ecclesiastical slang; and short texts on subjects as varied as legal actions taken against animals, the history of *la claque*—paid applauders—in the French theater, and the customs of wearing a tuxedo. The mind rummaging through all this is there in the poems too, naming, sometimes with an obscure synonym, the particulars of its one and only world.

That world has attracted a number of translators, yet Follain seems to remain, in the US, and even in France, as a Parisian bookseller once said to me, "highly regarded and little known." I first came across Follain in an anthology of W.S. Merwin's translations. Merwin translated and published a selection of Follain's poems in 1969 called *Transparence of the World* (its title drawn from a volume of Follain's), which was reissued in 2003. But it doesn't contain any poems from Follain's final book, nor any of his prose poems. Heather McHugh's 1981 translation of the volume *D'Après Tout* is now out of print, as is William Matthews and Mary Feeney's 1979 selection of Follain's prose poems, *A World Rich in Anniversaries.* More recently published were Kurt Heinzelman's *Demarcations* (2011), a translation of Follain's book *Territoires*; Christopher Middleton's broader selection, *130 Poems*, published in the UK (2010); and Ciaran Carson's *From Elsewhere* (2014), a hybrid volume offering a number of Follain translations with Carson's own poems in response.

My selection, which is arranged chronologically, favors poems that have not already been translated into English; exceptions were unavoidable. I have also included a number of prose poems from *Tout Instant*, making this the first volume in English to offer poems from all of Follain's books. All rationales aside, I translated the poems that I love, hoping others might love them too.

*—Andrew Seguin*

## The Three Brothers

*To Max Jacob*

One shuts the window giving on to morning glories
and removes the layers of clothing from his sick child,
his heart will come of age
in his innards he hears the rumbling
that comes from digesting white meat.
His two brothers enter a foreign land
and look for someplace warm
at the edge of the train station
without at all seeing the stars;
in threadbare bags they are carrying architectural plans
and their long fingers gnawed by acids
have never known love except in dreams,
the village clay sticks to their black shoes.

## Les Trois Frères

*À Max Jacob*

L'on ferme la fenêtre donnant sur les liserons
et l'on retire ses panoplies à l'enfant malade,
son cœur va mûrir
dans ses entrailles il entend la rumeur que fait
la digestion des viandes blanches.
Ses deux frères entrent sur la terre étrangère
et cherchent l'endroit chaud aux abords de la gare
sans rien voir des étoiles ;
dans de mauvais sacs ils portent des plans d'architecture
et leurs grands doigts rongés par les acides
n'ont guère connu l'Amour qu'en rêve,
l'argile du village colle à leurs souliers noirs.

## Shadows

Two men are arguing
and their reasons are alcohol,
a child buckles the belt
on a jacket flecked with dried mud,
at his side a tree shivers;
old lees stagnate near
the paneled door of the distillers
and a stench of fish
floats at the edges of the bright convent.
Farmers make kisses clap
on the cheeks of their lively pale daughters
who turn the compost;
a priest is rubbing his plowman's hands
first one then the other
gloved in old reddish black gloves
and the protagonist of dreams
drinks wine heavy with myrtle and cypress
out of a glass cut
right from his icy heart.

# Ombres

Deux hommes discutent
et leurs raisons sont celles de l'alcool,
un enfant boucle son ceinturon
sur un sarrau maculé de boue sèche,
à son côté frissonne un arbre ;
de vieilles lies stagnent près du vantail des distilleries
et des relents de poisson
flottent aux abords du clair couvent.
Les maraîchers font claquer des baisers
sur les joues de leurs filles aux pâleurs vivantes
qui soignent des terreaux ;
un prêtre frotte l'une à l'autre
ses mains de laboureur
gantées d'anciens gants noirs rougis
et le personnage des rêves
boit d'un vin lourd de myrte et de cyprès
dans une coupe taillée
à même les glaces de son cœur.

## Landscape of the End of Day

Their hands steady and vegetal
all day the dress fitters
bent like gleaners
adjusted the hems of gowns
and the glove makers hunched over gloves,
again the sky will wrap them gently in its shawl
some of them are heartbroken
the water rinsing their tired arms
splays in silver ripples.
In the elementary street of Air and Fire
their eyes cross children's hoops
that describe a perfect circle
and the sweet sister of a bar girl
who holds starred bottles to her heart
while the dice fall.

## Paysage de fin de journée

D'une main ferme et végétale
les essayeuses tout le jour
ployées comme des glaneuses
ont ajusté le bas des robes
et les gantières au front penché le gant,
le ciel va les reprendre dans sa douceur d'écharpe,
d'aucunes sont brisées d'amour,
l'eau qui baigne leurs bras fatigués
se creuse en rides d'argent.
Dans la rue élémentaire d'Air et de Feu
leurs yeux croisent les cerceaux d'enfant
qui dessinent un cercle parfait
et la douceur sœur d'une fille d'estaminet
qui presse sur son cœur des bouteilles étoilées
alors que tombent les dés.

## Long Week

To hear in the depths of memory
the creaking of doors in cold rooms
while poplars rustled on the riverbanks
is to feel one's blood thrill;
in summer the milk soured over red coals
the guard beat a drum in the heart of town
hornets flew from a blue corner
a little girl cried out
at being given white gloves,
in a fold of her dress
a kernel of wheat had fallen
which bestowed its frail shadow
and the toothed wheels of the coffee mills
turned beneath high dark ceilings.

# Longue semaine

En entendant grincer au fond de la mémoire
les portes des salles froides
lorsque bruissaient les peupliers des rives
on sent s'émerveiller son sang ;
l'été le lait tournait sur les charbons rougis
le garde battait la caisse au cœur de bourg
des frelons s'envolaient d'un coin bleu
une petite fille criait
pour l'introduction de gants blancs,
dans un pli de sa robe
un grain de blé était tombé
qui prodiguait son ombre frêle
et les meules dentées des moulins à café
tournaient sous les hauts plafonds noirs.

## Summer in Paris Under the Second Empire

*To André Salmon*

Set beside the child in the park
to whom it is taught
that Judas hung himself
is a lacquered coin chest
that opens with a miniscule key;
nearby a tree's in silence
its shadow covers a dead bird;
the rays of a dominant sun
light up the money box;
between a girl's teeth cherry pulp
spreads its dark crimson juice;
a black lattice gate keeps
the innocent pig in its pen
at the neighborhood fattener's near Poissonière,
the squires are downcast
in tall white hats and white breeches,
dye brightens the old man's sideburns
and two blue porters
gossip near a streetlamp.

# Été de Paris sous le second Empire

*À André Salmon*

À côté de l'enfant du square
à qui l'on apprend
que Judas se pendit
on a posé la tirelire vernie
qu'ouvre une clef minuscule ;
tout près c'est un arbre en silence
son ombre couvre un oiseau mort,
les rayons d'un soleil majeur
illuminent la boîte à sous ;
une pulpe de cerise entre des dents de fille
répand son jus cramoisi sombre ;
une claie noire retient
le porc innocent dans sa bauge
chez le nourrisseur du quartier Poissonnière ;
les écuyers sont tristes
haut chapeautés et culottés de blanc,
la teinture avive les favoris du vieux
et deux portefaix bleus
près d'un réverbère causent.

## Landscape of Rural Hardship

Fruit falls softly on the clenched earth
and the old man
in the too-short cloak of a child
follows the path
taking tiny steps to its end.
A small garden of chives
trembles beneath the stars.
At the house by the turnoff
a blue wheel leans on the wall,
the wheelwright and his workers
form, as they eat standing up, a silent group
seemingly waiting to reduce
through one final effort
the misery and fear in the world.

## Paysage de rurale douleur

Des fruits tombent doucement sur la terre serrée
et le vieillard
au trop court capuchon d'enfant
suit le chemin
d'un pas menu jusqu'à l'extrême.
Un petit jardin de cives
tremblote sous les étoiles.
À l'habitation du tournant
une roue bleue au mur s'appuie,
le charron et ses aides
forment, mangeant debout, un groupe muet
semblant attendre pour réduire
dans un dernier effort
la misère et la peur du monde.

# The Beer Drinker

It's the reader of detective novels
who also translated the Homeric epics;
he watches his glass redden
in the great sundown of Europe.
There are vapors wandering everywhere
which must be untangled;
there are men with organs full of holes, eaten up,
with radiating cancers
and all along the paths
these furrows of black earth where some dog dies.
Man of the North, he slowly drinks
a strong dark beer
whose bitterness goes well with the old gilded décor
and in a measured way
he grasps the handle of the mug
and brings it to his lips
this former schoolboy stained with violet ink,
he used to parade around
sticking out his illuminated tongue
in the courtyard in July
the lindens already yellow.

## Le Buveur de biére

C'est le lecteur de romans policiers
qui pourtant traduisit les longs récits d'Homère ;
il voit son bock qui rougeoie
au grand coucher d'Europe.
Il y a partout de rôdantes vapeurs
qu'il faudrait délier ;
il y a des hommes aux organes minés, troués,
aux cancers éclatants
et le long des chemins
ces sillons de terre noire où meurt quelque chien.
Homme du Nord, il boit lentement
une très forte bière
dont l'amer s'allie bien à l'or des vieux décors
et c'est avec mesure
qu'il prend l'anse du verre,
l'approche de ses lèvres
d'ancien collégien taché d'encre violette,
il paradait alors
montrant sa langue enluminée
dans la cour de Juillet aux tilleuls déjà jaunes.

## Hardware Store

In a retail hardware store in the country
men come to select
screws and nuts
and their hair is gray and their hair is red
or it's straight or sticking up.
The wide shop fills with a bluish air,
in its smell of iron
young women give off
the scents of their bodies.
It's enough to touch bolts or forged crosses
for sale there untouched
to feel the heft of the inevitable world.

And so the hardware store sails toward the eternal
selling its fill
of great gleaming nails.

# Quincaillerie

Dans une quincaillerie de détail en province
des hommes vont choisir
des vis et des écrous
et leurs cheveux sont gris et leurs cheveux sont roux
ou roidis ou rebelles.
La large boutique s'emplit d'un air bleuté,
dans son odeur de fer
de jeunes femmes laissent fuir
leur parfum corporel.
Il suffit de toucher verrous et croix de grilles
qu'on vend là virginales
pour sentir le poids du monde inéluctable.

Ainsi la quincaillerie vogue vers l'éternel
et vend à satiété
les grands clous qui fulgurent.

## Masons of 1830

Placid the masons from La Creuse
in long silent bands
crossed back through Paris in the evening
to their dormitories of bunks
without seeing the displays
of fatty salmon
frothy gowns
gold and colored gemstones,
they were daydreaming of returning to their lands
of vipers and sinkholes
as they passed pale dandies dressed
in beautiful aubergine and ivy fabrics.
Builders of new palaces
they headed back in slow troops
to their daily gathering around the table
when each in his own turn lifted
through shreds of twilight
the bowl of thick soup.

## Les Maçons de mil huit cent trente

Placides les maçons de la Creuse
en longues bandes silencieuses
retraversaient Paris le soir
jusqu'à leurs dortoirs de barrière
et sans voir aux étalages
gras saumons
robes écumeuses
ors et pierres de couleur,
rêvassaient du retour à leurs terres
de vipères et de fondrières,
croisaient les pâles dandys vêtus
de beaux draps aubergine et lierre.
Façonniers de nouveaux palais
en troupeaux lents ils retournaient
vers l'attablement journalier
quand chacun soulève à son tour
dans les lambeaux du crépuscule
la terrinée de soupe épaisse.

## The Fox

Prowling sometimes in our nights is a fox
who on the sleeping earth
is looking to feed dangerously
brushing past the sweet leaf
and from a long dream of thievery
of childhood and shame
filled yet with the mysteries of warm bread
and hot fires in thatched cottages
with throats parched we wake.

## Le Renard

Dans nos nuits parfois rôde un renard
qui sur la terre dormante
cherche un vivre hasardeux
frôlant la feuille sucrée
et d'un long rêve de rapines
d'enfance et de honte
empli pourtant des mystères du pain chaud
et du feu ardent des chaumières
l'on s'éveille la gorge altérée.

## The Last Aurochs

Near an ocean without sails
but bubbling with monsters
over the warm body
of the last aurochs to give up breath
snouts leaned in to devour it.
Their eyes were less cold
than the blues in the child impaling a fly
with the hairpin forgotten by his mother
gone to the appointment
in the stilted and delicate apparel
of misbegotten daughters.

## Le Dernier Auroch

Près d'un océan sans voiliers
mais bossué de monstres
sur le chaud cadavre
du dernier auroch expiré
des museaux se penchèrent et pour le dévorer.
Leurs yeux étaient moins froids
que ceux bleus de l'enfant traversant une mouche
avec l'épingle qu'oublia sa mère
partie au rendez-vous dans l'appareil guindé
et délicat des filles d'amour.

## City Outskirts

Maids insult each other
from one garden to the next
seeming to defend their masters' roses,
the startled girl
having broken some dark ornament
studies her wounded leg
and the children's war carries on
to the foot of a cross.
At the slaughterhouse the butcher kills the lamb
and a cracked bottle is tossed outside
which for a long time will keep its violet-blue dregs.

## Confins des villes

Des servantes s'injurient
d'un jardin à l'autre
qui semblent de leurs maîtres défendre les roses,
la vierge alarmée
ayant cassé un bibelot sombre
contemple sa jambe blessée
et la bataille d'enfants se poursuit
au pied d'une croix.
À l'abattoir le boucher tue l'agneau
et l'on jette dehors la bouteille fêlée
qui gardera longtemps son dépôt violet-bleu.

## Walled Courtyard

He is alone in the walled courtyard
with a toy that beats
on a worn-out spring
a feather takes flight
which is coming back
to land on the ground
where the armies of love
and the armies of fear
are pitted against one another.
The wall sparkles
its top is covered
in thick green bottle shards
for keeping out thieves.

## La Cour murée

Il est seul dans la cour murée
avec un jouet dont bat
le ressort fatigué
une plume s'envole
qui s'en vient retomber
sur la terre où s'affrontent
les forces de l'amour
celles aussi de la peur.
Le mur étincelle
son faîte est recouvert
de ces gros tessons verts
arrêtant les voleurs.

## Friends from Austerlitz

The troubled blacksmiths
close friends from Austerlitz
ate woodpigeons
without speaking a word,
they were neighbors on the river
and loved the brambles
surrounding their land;
they built tall fires
that lit up their nights
in which trees shook
in gusts of wind
and hand in hand
watched the same dawn.

# Les Amis d'Austerlitz

Les forgerons soucieux
grands amis d'Austerlitz
mangeaient les palombes,
ils ne parlaient pas
et riverains du fleuve
aimaient la ronce
entourant leur enclos ;
ils faisaient de grands feux
qui brillaient dans leurs nuits
où les arbres tremblaient
dans les chasses du vent
et la main dans la main
regardaient la même aube.

## History

As history seems
sad to the world at times
the heavy dinner gets cold
the great orator never returns
his mistress follows her dreams
later on
it's the uprooting
the muffled gunshots
the bells of a grand congress
on which night falls
while out in the fields
of his eternal childhood
the poet is walking
not wanting to forget a thing.

# L’Histoire

Comme l’histoire au monde
par moments apparaît triste
le dîner lourd refroidit
le tribun ne revient pas
sa maîtresse suit ses rêves
plus tard
c’est l’arrachement
la fusillade étouffée
les cloches d’un grand congrès
sur lequel la nuit tombe
alors que dans les champs
de son enfance éternelle
le poète se promène
qui ne veut rien oublier.

# Peace

A thug called Cheater of Death
a girl who bruised beneath his blows
came to a city built of sand and whitewash
in a block of time
nineteen hundred and ten
to live and die.
Smoke-colored top hats
appeared in the lifeless streets.
A man called out to his brother
a woman killed herself for love
a few people were predicting war
for a day.

## La Paix

Un voyou appelé Trompe-la-Mort
une fille que bleuissaient ses coups
sur une ville bâtie à chaux et à sable
dans un bloc du temps
mil neuf cent dix
arrivaient à vivre et mourir.
Les chapeaux hauts de forme
couleur de fumée
se voyaient dans les rues atones.
Un homme appelait son frère
une femme se tuait par amour
quelques-uns prédisaient la guerre
pour un jour.

## Day on Fire

The door shined in fiery daylight
but the braids of the women there
held still
one of them leaned over the waters of the cauldrons
and on a piece of porcelain
a painted bird had worn itself out with singing.
The messenger was seen to come in
with a letter and a golden loaf in his hands
he spoke
then it was dead silent
and the whole garden gave up its scent.

## La Journée en feu

La porte brillait dans le jour en feu
mais les nattes des habitantes
ne tremblaient pas
l'une se penchait sur les eaux des chaudrons
et peint sur une faïence
un oiseau s'épuisait à chanter.
On vit entrer le messager
il avait dans ses mains
une lettre et un pain d'or
il parla
puis ce fut un silence austère
et tout le jardin embauma.

# The Hour

The hour when the child stopped
to play with seashells
sparkled with the future
the smooth valves inside
held the scent of the sea
one could hear them chopping up
weeds for the animals
flies landed on the words
of the daily calendar
between watertight walls
and a sentence
let itself out
from between two lips
carrying through space in endless waves.

## L'Heure

L'heure où l'enfant s'arrêtait
de jouer avec des coquillages
étincelait de futur
les valves au dedans lisse
gardaient l'odeur de la mer
l'on entendait hacher
pour les bêtes les herbes amères
les mouches sur les mots
du calendrier des jours
se posaient entre les murs étanches
et la phrase
se détachait d'entre les lèvres
livrant à l'espace des ondes éternelles.

## Landscape with Two Laborers

The countryside was calm
a girl was washing her unblemished leg
and the hours
etched themselves into the cloth they faded
attacking the damask flowers.
The pages of a schoolbook
had been carried off by the wind
up above the eglantines
and down the length of the path
to ditches filled with clever beasts
to embankments covered in those herbs
favored for soothing teas
two laborers took their time
telling each other
the secrets of working with wood.

# Paysage des deux ouvriers

La campagne restait calme
une fille lavait sa jambe pure
et les heures
s'inscrivaient dans l'étoffe qu'elles usent
attaquant les fleurs dans le damas.
Les pages d'un livre d'école
avaient été par le vent emportées
jusqu'au-dessus des églantiers
et le long du chemin
aux fossés pleins de bêtes rusées
aux talus couverts de ces herbes propices
à des tisanes de douceur
deux ouvriers longuement se contaient
les secrets des métiers du bois.

## Durations

Veil spread over his head
when this man
photographed his beardless son
people were already saying
he had one foot
in his grave
women sought grass
for the voiceless rabbits
then came the mild weather
of the grape harvest
coal flared
in those great houses
where sometimes dark blood
dried beside a gold coin.

## Durées

Le voile étendu sur la tête
quand cet homme
photographiait son fils imberbe
les gens disaient déjà
qu'il était sur le bord
de sa tombe
des femmes cherchaient l'herbe
pour des lapins sans voix
puis venaient les douces vendanges
l'anthracite flambait
dans ces grands demeures
où parfois du sang noir séchait
près d'une pièce d'or.

## Shadows and Gleams

In the leafy shade of an enclosure
an entire world feeds
and the officer returns
with his uniform covered in black braids
a lobed leaf
trembles in the north wind
gripping the wooden table
with a square hand
a man goes on
surrounded by his bees
but the woman
crumbles flaky bread
for a circle of blessed birds.

## Ombres et Lueurs

Dans l'ombrage d'un clos
tout un monde dévore
et l'officier rentre
l'habit chargé de tresses noires
une feuille lobée
tremble au vent du nord
tenant le bois de table
d'une main carrée
résiste un homme
qu'entourent ses abeilles
mais la femme
émiette un pain friable
au cercle des oiseaux bénis.

## To the Country

They had decided to go out
to the country
where the same old woman
knits along the path
where the mother
lightly shakes the child
saying at her wit's end
will you hush up, will you hush up?
Then during the game the little girl
again says to her friend
you're getting warmer
and the other looks for so long
so late — O long life —
that soon the leaves are black.

## Au pays

Ils avaient décidé de s'en aller
au pays
où la même vieille femme
tricote sur le chemin
où la mère
secoue un peu l'enfant
lui disant à la fin des fins
te tairas-tu, te tairas-tu ?
Puis dans le jeu à son amie
la fillette redit tu brûles
et l'autre cherche si longtemps
si tard — ô longue vie —
que bientôt les feuilles sont noires.

# Police

From a police station giving on to a garden
beside a ditch
and a greenhouse
the bend in the road appears
studded with dark hemlocks
a bird lingers there
a flower droops
and the lengthy work goes on
with compass, ruler
and colored ink
striving night and day
to surround the world.

# Police

D'un bureau de police donnant sur un jardin
près d'une fosse
et d'une serre
le tournant de la route apparaît
orné de sombres ciguës
un oiseau s'y attarde
une fleur s'y penche
et le long travail se poursuit
avec règle et compas
et encre de couleur
qui nuit et jour s'efforce
à cerner le monde.

## Black Ants

Hands in his pockets he looks
at the world of black ants
their blood the color of lacquer
their pincers
their white larvae
quaking in the vibrations
of a bell
his beginner's violin is asleep in its case
and night is going to sow its stars
on the celestial map.

# Fourmis noires

Les mains aux poches il regarde
le monde des fourmis noires
leur sang couleur de laque
leurs aiguillons
leurs larves blanches
frémissantes aux vibrations
d'une cloche
son violon de jeune homme dort dans un coffre
et la nuit va semer ses étoiles
sur la carte céleste.

## In Those Times

At the time of the Sun King's
countless entourage
there had been a freeze
one night on the ground
the man after taking a drink
had wiped his blonde mustache
and the woman looked awhile
at crystals of frost
the coming centuries were waiting
a long army
on the mountaintops.

# Dans le temps

Au temps des innombrables suites
du roi Soleil
il avait gelé
une nuit sur la terre
l'homme après boire
avait essuyé sa moustache blonde
et la femme un peu regardé
les cristaux du givre
les siècles futurs attendaient
longue armée
au sommet des monts.

# Flowers

Flowers seem to be watching
huddled together in groups
along the edges of a ravine
and one can be afraid of these tufts
unsleeping in the loam,
not one miller not one dray
but the one sky
of a province
where sometimes a large bowl cracks
along its painted flowers.

# Des Fleurs

Des fleurs semblent regarder
groupées en nombres
sur les bords d'un ravin
et l'on peut avoir peur de ces touffes
à même le terreau
ne dormant pas,
aucun meunier aucun fardier
mais le seul ciel
d'une province
où parfois un grand bol se casse
à fleurs peintes.

# Eclogue

In the shuttered house
he stares at an object in the evening
and plays at the game of existing
a fruit trembles
at the back of the orchard
where scraps of pompous fashions
and the draped lacework
of the dead
float like a scarecrow from the tree
that is groaning in the wind
but on a lightning-struck oak
a bird is not afraid to sing
an old man has placed his hand
where a young heart
vowed obedience.

# Églogue

Dans la maison refermée
il fixe un objet dans le soir
et joue à ce jeu d'exister
un fruit tremble
au fond du verger
des débris de modes pompeuses
où pendent les dentelles
des morts
flottent en épouvantail à l'arbre
que le vent fait gémir
mais sur un chêne foudroyé
l'oiseau n'a pas peur de chanter
un vieillard a posé sa main
à l'endroit d'un jeune cœur
voué à l'obéissance.

## The Chouanne*

**Royalist insurgent of Western France, 1792-1800*

In the thick of the old world
having taken off all her apparel
and looked at her body
in the light
the chouanne rejoiced
and her gray horse whinnied
enclosed in the silent pen
serving history and magic
furnished with a heart and with lungs
and all that sky above them
would be the same for the assemblies
the same for stupefying wars.

## La Chouanne

Dans l'épaisseur du vieux monde
ayant enlevé toute parure
et regardant son corps
dans la lumière
exultait la chouanne
et son cheval gris hennissait
fixé dans l'enclos silencieux
servant l'histoire et la magie
pourvu d'un cœur et de poumons
et tout ce ciel au-dessus d'eux
serait celui des assemblées
et celui des guerres inouïes.

# Elimination

Grass has grown in the deep ditch
the man walking along stares
at the stretched-out cloud
fringed like his grey suit
dogs bark at the gaping horizons
each in its own way
although everything is at peace
the daylight will decline
again it will be necessary
to cut the bread at night
sitting on the rustic chopping block
with, when all is said and done,
unthinkable death.

## Effacement

L'herbe a grandi au fossé profond
l'homme en marchant fixe
le nuage étiré
frangé comme son habit gris
des chiens aux horizons béants
diversement aboient
pourtant c'est la paix
le jour va s'incliner
il faudra bien encore
couper le pain à la nuit
assis sur le billot rustique
avec en fin de compte
l'impensable mort.

## Under the Heavens

It was the farm with the beautiful cider press
the best-placed hearts
where singing voices carried
and lizards came along
all in an hour
that went on like a century of mankind.
The sound
a falling apple made
was heard by a child
drinking the milk of a stern woman
whose tan skin was marked
by moles and lines
in a pattern all its own
amongst the order of creatures.

## Sous les cieux

C’était la ferme au beau pressoir
aux cœurs les mieux placés
il en partait des voix chantantes
des lézards y venaient
toute une heure
qui durait comme un siècle d’homme.
Le bruit que fait
la chute d’une pomme
l’enfant l’entendait
en buvant le lait d’une femme
grave et marquée
sur sa peau hâlée
de grains et de lignes
d’une disposition unique
dans l’ordre des créatures.

## The Notice

The child pushing along the ring of a barrel
as his makeshift hoop
runs alone and shouts
but to the one who has just spelled out
beneath the N and the eagle of Empire
the draft notice
the old man says simply
in the blazing sun
while drinking a foamy pear cider:
"the next century will be worse"
though lovers go by singing.

# L'Affiche

L'enfant poussant un cercle de tonneau
qui lui sert de fruste cerceau
court seul avec des cris
mais à celui qui vient d'épeler
sous l'N et l'aigle de l'Empire
l'affiche de conscription
le vieillard seulement dit
dans l'embrasement du soleil
en buvant un poiré mousseux :
« le prochain siècle sera pire »
mais passent les amants qui chantent.

A song comes out of each object. The artisan has sealed up inside it a bit of his body, which had known love intimately, then had lived with disease for a long time, unless it was simply done in by old age. Song of wood, of steel, of copper. Across the centuries one can hear the executioners guffaw, the girls laugh in a wild voice, the madwomen bleat, the child warble. The object does not disappear. So many random things can be found in the pockets of travellers: pen knives, small notebooks, a miniscule screw forgotten during some disassembly, a twist of string, a few carrot or parsnip seeds, the same seeds that the man, when he was home and leaning over the earth, scattered into the furrow he'd dug in the planting bed of his enclosure. The horizon dissolves before the eyes of the walker. He's carrying so many secrets in his head, the afterlives of love, desires that are concrete for an instant but then evaporate, while the object, even if he has forgotten it, remains in his pocket like a talisman. Sorting one day through old clothes that our body, weighed-down and watched from afar by death, no longer fits, we find the cogwheel of a delicate machine and struggle to recall its use. We turn it over and over in our fingers while in the distance a storied sun goes down.

Un chant s'élève de chaque objet. L'artisan y a enfermé un peu de son corps qui avait bien connu l'amour, puis avait porté longtemps une maladie, à moins qu'il ne se fût simplement éteint de vieillesse. Chant du bois, de l'acier, du cuivre. On entend à travers les siècles ricaner les bourreaux, les filles rire d'une voix sauvage, les folles bêler, l'enfant gazouiller. L'objet ne s'évanouit pas. On trouve de si multiples choses dans les poches des voyageurs : des canifs, de petits carnets, une minuscule vis oubliée lors d'un démontage, un bout de ficelle entortillé, quelques graines de carottes ou de panais, de ces mêmes graines que l'homme, alors sédentaire et courbé vers la terre lançait dans le petit sillon qu'il avait creusé dans la plate-bande de l'enclos. Devant les yeux du promeneur, l'horizon se dilue. Lui, porte en tête maint secret, des restes d'amour, des désirs un moment consistants, mais qui s'évaporent tandis que l'objet, même s'il l'a oublié, reste en poche comme un talisman. Fouillant un jour les vieux vêtements dans lesquels notre corps alourdi et guetté, fût-ce de très loin par la mort, n'entre plus, on retrouve le rouage d'une frêle machine dont on doit faire effort pour retrouver l'usage. On le retourne longtemps entre ses doigts alors qu'au loin se couche un soleil d'histoire.

On the most beautiful evenings, the small objects that wear out so slowly, the ones that last until they are broken by accident, give in to being overrun by shadows and those insidious dusts carried in on the air. The mirror offers its renewable magic. Gathered in on itself, the house breathes. None of its inhabitants could say exactly what is hiding up there under its eaves amidst drying onions, sprouting potatoes, and an old science book going yellow and dry. Who had opened that book and seen in it devices engraved meticulously with minute hash marks forming the shadows. In one of the rooms of the house, you can hear through the wall someone scratching away at a splotch on a large sheet of white loose-leaf and blowing gently to scatter the tiny paper fibers shed during the procedure. Bottles of black and red ink keep vigil. An imitation Japanese begging bowl is full of pins. Binders, well-thumbed dossiers, still bear their titles and inscriptions long after the death of the people who made use of them on those days when all anyone wanted to do was stay inside as the storm raged so disastrously through delicate flowers.

Par les plus beaux soirs, les petits objets dont l'usure est si lente, ceux-là qui durent jusqu'à ce qu'un hasard les brise, se laissent envahir par les ombres et par ces poussières insidieuses que l'air charrie. La glace offre sa magie toujours neuve. Ramassée sur elle-même, la maison respire. Nul de ses habitants ne pourrait dénombrer exactement ce qui se cache sous ses combles au milieu des oignons qui sèchent, des pommes de terre qui germent et d'un vieux livre de sciences sec et jauni. Qui eût ouvert ce livre y eût vu des appareils méticuleusement gravés avec de petites hachures pour figurer les ombres. Dans une des pièces de la maison, on entend à travers le mur quelqu'un qui gratte une tache sur une grande feuille blanche et souffle doucement pour éparpiller la petite laine de papier issue de cette opération. Veillent la bouteille d'encre noire et celle d'encre rouge. Une sébille faussement japonaise contient des épingles. Des classeurs, des dossiers domestiqués gardent leur titres et inscriptions longtemps après la mort de ceux-là auxquels ils rendirent service ces jours que l'on veut rester chez soi tellement fait rage la tempête si néfaste aux fleurs fragiles.

A plank of the parquet floor creaks beneath two bare feet. The pendants of the chandelier clink a little then the grate of the fireplace shakes while the mantelpiece holds its black clock with roman numerals and serrated arms. Tirelessly, in his garden surrounded by hedges, a man is digging again to find treasure. The church clock chimes not only on the hours, but on the halves and the quarters, although he stops only on the hours and counts each stroke in his head. The world appears to him as the endless room of trials and experiments on which darkness falls, as it always has, each night.

Une lame de parquet gémit sous deux pieds nus. Les pendeloques du lustre tintent un peu puis vibre le rideau de la cheminée dont la tablette porte sa pendule noire à chiffres romains et à aiguilles dentelées. Inlassablement, dans son jardin entouré de haies, un homme refait des fouilles pour la découverte d'un trésor. L'horloge de l'église sonne non point seulement les heures, mais aussi les demies et les quarts mais il s'interrompt seulement aux heures et mentalement compte chaque coup. Le monde lui apparaît la vaste chambre d'expériences et d'épreuves sur laquelle l'ombre depuis toujours, chaque soir, descend.

Even as the sounds of war darken the world, we happen to come across, on the ground, a stained old postcard bearing a "Warmest Greetings" or a "Fondest Memories." This one shows quitting time at the national railroad factory in Saintes around 1910: men heading off every which way, going towards their soups cooked with the customary vegetables, picked from kitchen gardens with sagging fences, small tool sheds. Many of them wear those pelerine capes that make one dream of the monastic life. They don't seem to know they are under the camera's gaze. Everyone in the foreground is blurry. The surrounding houses would have been built around 1880. They will remain standing for a long time yet, but the uncertainty at the root of time is beginning to grow.

Même lorsque les bruits de guerre obscurcissent le monde, il nous arrive de trouver par terre une vieille carte postale maculée portant un « Affectueux bonjour » ou un « Meilleur souvenir ». Celle-ci représente la sortie des usines des chemins de fer de l'État à Saintes, vers 1910 : des hommes s'égaillent, allant vers des soupes garnies de légumes usuels, arrachés dans des jardinets à clôtures boiteuses, à petites cabanes à outils. Beaucoup portent de ces pèlerines qui font songer à l'état monastique. Ils n'ont pas l'air de savoir qu'ils sont sous l'objectif. Ceux du premier plan de la photographie sont flous. Les maisons environnantes ont dû être construites vers 1880. Certes, elles dureront encore longtemps, mais l'inquiétude au fond du temps s'amasse.

This most peculiar plant, whose bloom lasts for just a few hours, has begun to unfurl itself on the exact morning the owners of the garden have gone off somewhere. With striped petals, it sways in the breeze like other more common species. Everything is unbearably tender. In a shadowy corner is a colony built by corseted insects, worn gold. Nearby, people hastily go up steps; they come down. A hand stops along the banister of an oak staircase: each minute falls. By six o'clock this evening, the flower will be withered, the horizon going pale, and a group of girls singing without shyness or shame.

Cette plante si particulière, car la fleur n'en dure jamais que quelques heures, s'est mise à éclore ce matin que les propriétaires du jardin se sont absentés. De pétales tigrés, elle se balance aux brises comme tant d'autres plus communes. Tout est d'une terrible douceur. Dans un coin ombragé s'est établie une colonie d'insectes corsetés, vieil or. Aux alentours, on monte précipitamment des marches ; on les descend. Une main s'arrête sur la rampe d'un escalier de chêne : chaque minute tombe. A six heures du soir, la fleur sera flétrie, l'horizon commencera de pâlir, un groupe de jeunes filles de chanter sans faiblesse ni honte.

The road mender who gathers wilted flowers makes little piles of them. If one were to look in through the basement window, there would be the baker brushing his brioche with egg wash. High up on a rung of a tall extension ladder, a sign painter is meticulously beginning a capital letter beneath a furious sky in a scorching month.

A fountain with a grimacing grotesque atop it is no longer flowing. "Nothing to be done," a voice says from behind closed shutters. Between paving stones a plant has produced a yellow sprig that will maybe vanish without anyone having crushed it. The slightest chance at life is seized by these minuscule plants growing out of the cracks in the walls. Lead gutters show off their blue-grey. The blows of a hammer come from an alleyway, sounding out stationary work. Finally, wind comes off the hill where tombs rise up.

Le cantonnier qui ramasse les fleurs fanées en fait des petits tas. Si l'on regardait par le soupirail, on apercevrait un boulanger peindre des brioches à l'œuf battu. Monté sur un des hauts échelons d'une échelle double, un peintre en lettres commence une majuscule méticuleusement sous le ciel forcené d'un mois brûlant.

Une fontaine surmontée d'un mascaron grimaçant ne coule plus. « Rien à faire », dit une voix derrière des contrevents. Entre pavés, une plante a donné un herbe jaune qui peut-être finira sans que personne l'ait détruite. Gardent le plus chance de vie ces végétaux minuscules poussant aux fentes des murs. Des gouttières de plomb montrent leur bleu-gris. Dans un passage frappe un marteau manifestant un travail sédentaire. Enfin, le vent descend de la colline où s'élèvent des tombeaux.

It's a crossroads, treacherous they say. Quiet anyhow. A man has been seen there fashioning a whistle from softwood for a boy wearing a black jacket with impeccable pleats suggesting mourning or even a disguise, in a countryside where every leaf seems to have found its place forever ago. At each of the surrounding farms, the stew one eats has the same odor. On a tree trunk is a brittle auction notice posted on orders during a regime that was followed by a slightly bloodier one.

C'est un carrefour, traître à ce qu'on dit. Calme pourtant. On y a vu un homme confectionnant dans du bois tendre un sifflet à un garçon porteur d'un sarreau noir aux plis impeccables faisant deuil et même travesti, dans un paysage où chaque feuille semble à sa place de toute éternité. Dans chacune des fermes de l'alentour, le ragoût qu'on mange garde la même odeur. Sur un tronc d'arbre se voit l'affiche desséchée d'une vente aux enchères par ordre collée lors d'un régime que suivit un autre à peine plus sanglant.

In a country a custom deriving from English law remains, permitting anyone to cut through the fields to shorten their way. It's how the countrysides come alive. But doesn't it always happen that, thirsting for a chat with any living soul, a landowner calls out from his plot to the passerby on the blinding road. The conversation is about to unfold across that space. Then an already old dog goes by, hurrying faithfully down his appointed path, as if he must get to some urgent task in a universe that he has no idea will end, and which he makes, by his sudden presence, tip over into the unknown.

Dans un pays, l'usage demeure, venu du droit anglais, qui permet à un chacun de passer par les champs pour raccourcir son chemin. Ainsi sont animés les paysages. Mais n'arrive-t-il pas que, désireux de parler à âme qui vive, un propriétaire interpelle d'un pré carré le passant sur la route aveuglante. La conversation va se poursuivre à travers l'espace. Puis passe un chien déjà âgé poursuivant soucieux sa route à vive allure, comme s'il devait se rendre à quelque urgente occupation dans un univers qu'il ignore périssable, et fait, par sa subite présence, chavirer dans l'inconnu.

One evening at the beginning of this century a mathematician can be seen arriving to his home, carrying in his hand a bird cage that, absent-minded as most great thinkers are, he picked up without even realizing it from a display down at the quay of the bird catchers. Having been wending his way through the yellow and black horse cabs, he didn't see, down an alleyway, a dog fleeing with a leg of lamb in its jaws, pursued by a furious and mustachioed butcher. The memory of such farcical hours will tremble in the future. Citizens who will have survived massacres will be there with their arms crossed, on wicker chairs, again seeing the phantom professor in the well-brushed black frock coat holding his empty cage.

On voit un soir du début de ce siècle ce mathématicien arriver jusque chez lui ayant en main une cage à oiseau que, distrait à la manière des savants, il a sans qu'il s'en aperçoive prise à un étalage du quai des oiseleurs. Ayant cheminé à travers les fiacres jaunes et noirs, il n'a pas vu dans une ruelle un chien s'enfuir avec un gigot dans la gueule, poursuivi par un boucher furieux et moustachu. Dans l'avenir va trembler le souvenir de ces heures dérisoires. Des citoyens qui auront survécu aux massacres seront bras croisés, sur des chaises tressées, revoyant le fantôme du professeur en noir à redingote bien brossée tenant sa cage inhabitée.

In the kinds of houses one steps into hesitantly, one must, with the door left open, go up a staircase before reaching the only inhabited room. From below, the woman who is visiting calls out: "Are you there?" And the isolated woman answers: "Yes, I'm expecting you, come on up." The visitor slips off her shoes to not track in dirt. The wood of the staircase is about to creak beneath her feet. This is what it means to go out and see the world: it takes just a touch of ceremony. When the two of them are sitting face to face, they speak guardedly and their shadows lean toward one another on the bare whiteness of the wall. All around them, drying vegetation makes its presence felt: willow for baskets, the hazelnuts of a bygone summer, bunches of yellowing beans hanging until seedtime. Nothing special.

Dans des maisons où l'on entre avec précaution, il faut, la porte ouverte, monter un escalier avant que d'arriver à la pièce habitée. D'en bas, la visiteuse s'enquiert : « Êtes-vous là ? » Et l'habitante isolée répond : « Oui, je vous attends, montez. » Celle qui rend visite enlève alors ses sabots pour ne pas salir. Le bois de l'escalier va geindre sous son pas. C'est bien cela aller voir le monde : il faut y mettre un rien de cérémonie. Quand toutes deux sont assises face à face, elles parlent avec précaution et leurs ombres s'approchent sur la blancheur morte du mur. A l'entour d'elles, s'impose la sècheresse végétale : osier des paniers, noisettes d'un autre été, grappes de haricots jaunis suspendues pour la semence. Rien qui étonne.

## Instant

So many faces are
at the turnings
of a slow existence
beside the same windowpanes
welcoming the sun.
It's when the man goes by
his solid chest, his heavy legs
his smile
that it vibrates the most
the pure instant
of the one spike of wheat
picked by his carefree hand
making its escape from the scythe.

# Instant

Tant de visages sont
aux tournants
d'une lente existence
près des mêmes vitres
accueillantes au soleil.
C'est quand passe l'homme
sa poitrine solide, ses jambes alourdies
son sourire
que vibre le mieux
l'instant pur
du seul épi de blé
que sa main insoucieuse cueille
le faisant échapper à la faux.

## Blood

Finishing off the wounded
is the most unspeakable act
the trembling schoolchildren are told
while out in a garden
draped sheets are displayed
covered in the blood of the nuptials
that a murderer is fleeing
amidst bees
buckwheat, alfalfa stalks
with their purple clusters
beyond the celebrating village
the river is following
tinted bright pink
its course through the clays.

## Le Sang

Achever les blessés
le plus infâme geste
dit-on aux tremblants écoliers
cependant qu'un jardin
montre des linges étendus
couverts de sang nuptial
qu'un meurtrier fuit
au milieu des abeilles
du blé noir, des luzernes
à violets capitules
hors du village en fête
le fleuve poursuivant
teint de rose éclatant
son cours dans les argiles.

# The Fire

Ivy hung in long vines
from the gray house
of the metaphysician
fire took it one night
lighting up the cropped plain
ashes floated in the air
through the smell of burnt hay
then the heavens cleared
above the ruin overrun
by scores of motherless children
who played in its breaches
dressed in dark rags
imagining their long life.

## Le Feu

De grands lierres s'étiraient
sur la maison grise
du métaphysicien
le feu y prit une nuit
éclairant la plaine rase
dans l'air flottèrent les cendres
dans l'odeur du foin brûlé
puis les cieux passèrent calmés
sur la ruine assaillie
par beaucoup d'enfants sans mère
qui sur ses brèches jouèrent
vêtus de haillons noircis
imaginant leur vie longue.

# Artisans

Artisans full of order
make the most of time
that slips through their fingers
one reworks tirelessly
the circle and the hexagon
in the long evening;
the other has finished oiling the harnesses
his child is asleep
in the wicker crib;
the most skilled of them all
believes in wearing down death at best
letting the shadows spread out
on the festival square
without forcing dreams.

## Artisans

Les artisans pleins d'ordre
savent combler l'heure
qui s'évanouit sous leurs doigts
tel refait inlassable
le cercle et l'hexagone
dans le soir libéral ;
l'autre a fini de noircir les harnais
son enfant s'endort
dans le berceau à l'osier sec ;
le plus habile
croit fatiguer la mort au mieux
laisse s'étendre les ombres
sur la place des fêtes
sans forcer les songes.

## The Team

Throughout this old empire
whenever the coachman was going
holding the reins
he felt his beasts
foaming with sweat in the evening
while the stones flew
between warring brothers
in scrubby tangles of the world.
Sometimes having
vast wheat fields in sight
the team stopped.
With their long whinnies
in the docile coolness
the famished mares
woke lovers up
from their light sleep
beneath a sky full of mists.

## L’Attelage

Par cet ancien empire
quand allait le cocher
tenant les rênes
il sentait ses bêtes écumer dans le soir
alors volaient des pierres
entre frères ennemis
dans les maquis du monde.
Ayant parfois en vue
de vastes terres à blé
l’attelage s’arrêtait.
Hennissant longuement
dans la fraîcheur docile
les juments affamées
réveillaient des amants
de leur sommeil léger
sous un ciel de brumes.

## Shop

Men come to pick up
with a slow smile
wrapped packages
sometimes a white candle
in this spare shop
where decorated clogs hang
their voices call out:
"Anyone here?"
Finally a woman comes
to help them with her hands
having picked grass
from the sides of those paths
crossed so quickly
by a species of common hare.

## Boutique

Des hommes viennent chercher
avec un lent sourire
des paquets clos
parfois une bougie blanche
dans cette boutique austère
où pendent les sabots ornés
leur voix clame :
« Y a-t-il du monde ? »
Une femme vient enfin
les servir de ses mains
ayant cueilli l'herbe
au bord de ces chemins
que traverse si vite un lièvre
d'espèce commune.

## Anguish

Luminous skin moves
over the fine bones
of a slender woman
who looks at the boat full
of still living fish
at the bottom of an old powder barrel
the snail sleeps
but the baker will let the bread burn
a messenger with a striking profile
just before dawn
will hurt himself on a jagged stone.

## Angoisse

Une peau lumineuse bouge
sur le fin squelette
d'une femme élancée
qui regarde la barque pleine de poissons
pas morts encore
au fond d'un ancien baril à poudre
l'escargot dort
mais le boulanger laissera brûler le pain
un messager au beau profil
peu avant l'aube
se blessera sur la pierre angulaire.

## In Humans

In humans
sometimes a balance
of good nature is reached
as the smoke rises
a day laborer carrying back his scythe
while hammering the ground
reaches the hamlet colored like burnt bread
where with half-closed eyes his daughters rest.
On each face of the same rock
the insects of a floating world sleep.

## Chez l'homme

Chez l'homme
parfois se manifeste
une égalité d'humeur douce
alors montent les fumées
un journalier rapportant sa faux
en martelant le sol
va jusqu'au hameau couleur de pain brûlé
les yeux mi-clos ses filles s'y reposent.
Sur chaque face d'un même rocher
dorment les insectes
du monde léger.

# Dogs

Barking dogs silent dogs
on alert from morning till night
at the entranceway or along the streets
remain standing, sitting, lying down
often with a bloodshot eye.
A Newfoundland without knowing it
carries his island name and searches
through the mountains.
Great Danes like their masters trail on their backs
the gleam of yellow lamps
that light up and flicker
on a windy evening
full of troubles.

## Des chiens

Les chiens aboyants ou muets
du matin à la nuit qui s'effare
à l'entrée ou au long des rues
restent debout, assis, couchés
l'œil veiné souvent de sang.
Un terre-neuve sans savoir
porte son nom d'île et cherche
dans les montagnes.
Des danois comme leurs maîtres traînent au dos
le reflet de lampes jaunes
qui s'allument et tremblent
par un soir venteux
chargé de peines.

## The Woodpecker's Meal

Tending to have
sharp tongues
the women said nothing further
for the moment
infinitesimal seeds
fell upon their cool skin
and their shabby woolens
they were listening
to the beak of the woodpecker
tapping the thick bark
of a tall pine
making insects come out
for its evening meal.
But other birds arrived
they smiled together
then got back to talking loudly.

## Repas du pic-vert

Ayant disposition
à l'aigreur de la langue
elles ne disaient pourtant plus rien
des graines infimes
tombaient sur leur peau rafraîchie
et leurs lainages pauvres
elles écoutaient
le bec du pic-vert
frapper sur une écorce drue
de haut sapin
en faisant sortir les insectes
pour son repas du soir.
Mais arrivèrent d'autres oiseaux
elles en sourirent ensemble
puis se reprirent à parler fort.

## Injured Horse

In a room lit
by an opaque window
the fear of space and time is born.
That the heart of an injured horse
still beats
moves a gentle plowman
who cares for it and moans;
in its lone field the animal
slept standing up
for all of its nights.
Its owner knew not to give it
any more meaning
than needed for History.

## Cheval blessé

Dans la pièce qu'éclaire
un jour de souffrance
naît la peur de l'espace et du temps.
Que le cœur d'un cheval blessé
batte toujours
émeut un laboureur paisible
qui le soigne et plaint ;
l'animal dans le champ unique
dormait debout
ses nuits entières.
Son maître savait ne point donner
plus de sens
qu'il n'en faut à l'Histoire.

## The Plant

Wild species said to be noxious
it points towards the sky
its fluted stem and large umbels
sap rises bitter in its veins.
The emaciated man walking along
ready for war
tramples similar triumphant vegetation;
then hearing all the shouts of children
who are playing in the mist
he has had enough
of living and misusing it all.

## La Plante

Espèce sauvage dite nuisible
elle dresse sur le ciel
sa tige cannelée et ses grandes ombelles
la sève monte amère en ses canaux.
Le promeneur émacié
bon pour la guerre
abat pareil végétal triomphant ;
percevant alors tous ces cris des enfants
qui jouent dans les brumes
il n'en peut plus
de vivre et mésuser de tout.

# Forgetting

Countrysides soak up ancient sun
although the past
will never come back the same
the astute women
who want to forget
as much as they can
wear out their bodies beautifully
waving their supple arms
on a day that would like to stay calm.
Who could ever fix it
so that a child hadn't been hit by a stone
when at the back of the garden
beneath slow-moving clouds
out of neglect a tool has been left on the ground?

# Oubli

Des paysages reçoivent un soleil de jadis
le passé pourtant
ne reviendra jamais au même
les femmes adroites
qui veulent oublier
le plus qu'elles peuvent
fatiguent leur corps en beauté
agitent leurs souples bras
par un jour qui voudrait rester calme.
Qui pourra jamais faire
qu'un enfant n'ait été frappé par une pierre
quand au fond d'un jardin
sous des nuages lents
un outil par mégarde est resté sur la terre ?

# The Worth of Bread

Listening with his hands on the table
where the insects crawl
someone sees time wince
the russet plain spreads wide
with its dried-up river
the pleasures of the flesh have gone by
night falls fast
bringing its probing lamps
nothing remains
but the worth of bread
with white eyes
from which a slice is taken
in the dark.

# Valeur du pain

Écoutant les mains sur la table
où des bêtes marchent
quelqu'un voit le temps grimacer
la plaine rousse s'étend
avec sa rivière asséchée
le plaisir de chair a passé
la nuit vient vite
avec ses lampes probantes
il ne subsiste plus
que la valeur du pain
aux yeux blancs
qu'entame un tranchet
dans une pénombre.

# Humanity

Brown-haired men work
in sulfur or silver mines
to sleep at night in houses
with exposed beams
in the bare room their animals
go through the door left half-open
towards the dying fire
while from the ceiling onions
twist a little in russet garlands
but the children of another world
run with their parents beneath the downpour
to reach cover
and grow a little older there in the meantime.

## Humanité

Des hommes bruns travaillent
dans les mines de soufre ou d'argent
pour au soir dormir dans des maisons
à poutres visibles
leurs animaux dans la pièce austère
par la porte entr'ouverte exprès
vont vers le feu mourant
alors qu'au plafond des oignons
tremblent un peu en guirlandes rousses
cependant les enfants d'un autre monde
courent avec leurs parents sous l'averse
pour atteindre un refuge
et vieillir un peu dans l'attente.

## Gleaners

Some villages
with their extinguished forge
expand so quickly
in their love of gold
there are still two gleaners
who don't know what to say
seeing the same pearled clouds
on the horizon;
cracks run across
their palms
which the dirt fills in
and their dresses
are no longer black.

## Glaneuses

Des villages
avec leur forge éteinte
si vite s'agrandissent
dans leur amour de l'or
il reste deux glaneuses
qui ne savent quoi dire
voyant à l'horizon
les mêmes nuages perle ;
sur leurs paumes se croisent
des sillons
que la terre emplit
et leurs robes
ne sont plus noires.

## Anxiety

Clouds pass over the precipice
as the fields go dark
in the silence of the evening
and the fire shovel
falling on the stone
sends a fright through the countrywoman
who out of anxiety
makes a bouquet
of flowers and leaves
then softly sings
in memory
of her favorite son.

# L'Anxiété

Au-dessus du précipice
passent des nuées
lorsque s'assombrissent les champs
dans le silence de veillée
que la pelle à feu
en tombant sur la pierre
fait frémir la paysanne
qui dans l'anxiété
fait un bouquet
de fleurs et feuilles
puis faiblement chante
en souvenir
de son fils le meilleur.

# Return

Covered in whitewash
with wrinkles around his eyes
having set a bag of tools
against the grainy wall
the workman thinks back on his century
sees the beds remade
in a strict regime
a pile of iron
absorbs the growing night
the air brings
a light breeze
to the early plants
that will hold out until
their inconspicuous death.

## Retour

Couvert de chaux
des rides autour de ses yeux
ayant posé un sac d'outils
contre le mur grumeleux
l'ouvrier pense à son siècle
voit les lits refaits
dans la stricte ordonnance
un tas de ferraille
reçoit la nuit montante
l'air apporte
un léger souffle
aux végétaux hâtifs
qui résistent à leur mort
sournoise.

## Earthly Things

The foundation
riddled with animals
of the house by the side of the road
keeps its faithful walls up
chicken coops, rabbit hutches
beehives widowed or full
stretch to the end of the horizon
friends, enemies and the indifferent
gone astray or united by their footsteps
uncover leafy detours
prudent shortcuts
crossroads with tall grass
and sometimes go looking in full sun
for bravery.

# Appareil de la terre

Les fondations
pleines de bêtes
de la maison du bord de route
font résister ses murs loyaux
poulaillers, clapiers
ruches pleines ou veuves
s'étendent au fond des horizons
amis, ennemis et des indifférents
égarés, réunis par leurs pas
retrouvent détours feuillus
raccourcis de prudence
carrefours à l'herbe haute
et parfois cherchent au grand soleil
la bravoure.

## Walking

Stained linens
flap at the back of the fields
where the wheat hardens
the dog follows along
full of life
that will end certainly
before its master's;
both of them drag their shadows
sometimes looking at one another
when the roads cross
in a strange peace
where that time survives
beneath a final ray of sun.

## Marche

Des linges tachés
claquent au fond des terres
où se durcit le blé
le chien poursuit
une robuste vie
qui finira certes
avant celle du maître :
tous deux traînent leurs ombres
parfois se regardant
quand les routes se croisent
dans une étrange paix
où survit la durée
sous un rayon dernier.

## The Corncrake

The corncrake
during the time of its migrations
is always running
even if war cannons boom
it is only to pass over the pond
that it will open its russet wings.
At the end of an old world
slicing his bread
through the dormer he sees it clearly
this lone man safe and sound
who never once wanted to cry
but watches who goes past
up until the hour
set aside for prayer.

## Le Râle des genêts

Le râle des genêts
dans le temps de ses migrations
court toujours
même si tonnent les canons d'une guerre,
c'est seulement pour traverser l'étang
qu'il ouvrira ses ailes rousses.
Dans cette fin d'un monde ancien
découpant son pain
par sa lucarne le voit bien
cet homme seul abrité
qui jamais ne voulut pleurer
mais regarde qui passe
jusqu'à l'heure
que l'on dit la prière.

# Black Rain

The friends of a time
are still together
the houses are there
with their soots and vapors
bodies go off
along hidden paths
where the branches shake
the grass that was crushed
by yesterday's wagons
stands back up a little
then a black rain comes
over the aging lands
a passerby asks
has the hour struck?

## Pluie noire

Les amis d'un temps
restent réunis
les maisons sont là
leurs suies et vapeurs
des corps se déplacent
par chemins perdus
où tremblent les branches
l'herbe qu'écrasèrent
les charrois d'hier
se redresse un peu
puis vient la pluie noire
sur les terres vieillies
un passant demande
l'heure est-elle passée ?

## Animal at Evening

Surrounded by stone
the unspeaking animal waits
eyes fixed on the sea
a human sound
fills the harsh expanse
the heat arrives
in stiff cloth the woman
will play with the beast
as the sun goes down
both of them breathing
with the vegetal world
as a constellated night comes on.

## L’Animal au soir

Sur un fond de pierre
l’animal sans voix
attend l’œil ouvert sur le large
un bruit humain
emplit l’étendue âpre
la chaleur arrive
avec l’étoffe roide
la femme devant le couchant
va jouer avec la bête
tous deux respirent
avec le monde végétal
à l’approche d’une nuit constellée.

## Old Fortuneteller

Lovers take off
who can't be held back;
sundown spreads
across violet clouds
a farmwoman walks along
carrying a tart of green fruit
on her aging head
in the hamlet
of closed shutters
the middle of the century has passed;
sitting on an embankment
an old man who tells fortunes
and is soon to die
hardly sings anymore.

## Vieux devin

Des enamourés s'en vont
qu'on ne retient plus ;
le couchant s'étale
en stratus violine
une fermière avance
portant une tourte à fruits verts
sur sa tête vieillie
dans le hameau
à persiennes closes
le milieu du siècle a passé ;
assis sur un talus
un vieux devin
qui va bientôt mourir
ne chante plus qu'à peine.

# Figure of Time

At the shabby restaurant
one is without knowing it
beside an old killer
who studies
the woman who serves him
dressed in plain fabric.
She takes her stroked body home
puts on slippers and opens
with both of her hands
the window on to night
staying a moment
to peer at the leaves
that barely stir, a figure of Time.

## Figure du temps

Au restaurant pauvre
on est sans le savoir
près d'un vieil assassin
qui contemple
celle qui le sert
vêtue d'étoffe unie.
Elle rentre son corps caressé
met des chaussons et ouvre
de ses deux mains
la fenêtre sur la nuit
reste un moment
épiant les feuillages
à peine remués, figure du Temps.

## Through the Window

Through a window one sees
weights and measures
a dead man on his bed
the ward of wet nurses
where men examine
from behind their spectacles
swollen breasts.
What is the soul?
the weary priest puts forth
beneath a blazing sun
the boy answers wrong
preferring a slingshot
for wounding wild birds.

## Par la fenêtre

On voit par une fenêtre
des poids et mesures
un mort sur son lit
le bureau des nourrices
où des hommes examinent
derrière leur lorgnon
des poitrines gorgées.
Qu'est-ce que l'âme ?
interroge le prêtre las
sous un soleil intense
le garçon répond mal
préférant d'une fronde
blesser les oiseaux fauves.

# Power of Things

The enclosure reddens
flags lose their color
a faithful hand
with a steel-tipped wooden compass
traces a complete circle
on a plain sheet of paper.
Someone counts in his head
it is all there
in sun and mists
instruments and table
by the power of things.

## Force des choses

L'enclos rougeoie
des drapeaux pâlissent
une main loyale
d'un compas en bois à pointe d'acier
sur une feuille unie
trace un cercle entier.
Quelqu'un mentalement compte
tout reste là
au soleil et brumes
instruments et table
par la force des choses.

## Green Countryside

A frail girl
and the boy she leads
see the intense green flourishing:
the man who hunts nettles
is cutting them up with some bran
for the poultry with bloodshot eyes
not one leaf takes flight.
At the lively crossroads
someone stops and drinks
to the deep daylight
then finds the path
that leads furthest away.

## Vert paysage

Une fille fragile
et le fils qu'elle mène
voient s'épanouir le vert intense :
le chercheur d'orties
les hache avec le son
pour la volaille aux yeux sanglants
pas une feuille ne vole.
Au carrefour vibrant
quelqu'un s'arrête et boit
à la faveur du jour profond
puis trouve le chemin
qui va le plus loin.

## Wounds

A plant is ripped from the wall
by the thrown stone
of a careful sneak
a woman lets a linen drop
from her damp hand
falls asleep
with her breast wounded
the wind shakes
a rotting swing
a word comes to the surface
only to leave again for oblivion
vapors rise from the sheltered earth.

# Blessures

Une plante de muraille se déchire
sous le coup de caillou
d'un sournois vigilant
une femme laisse tomber
un linge
d'une main moite
s'endort la gorge blessée
le vent secoue une balançoire
pourrissante
un mot revient à la surface
pour repartir dans l'oubli
des vapeurs montent de la terre abritée.

# Equivocal

Equivocal to find beautiful again
some worn-out silent
things
a stone is there
hard and veined
it's poetry someone says
he has had enough of
a peal of laughter can be made out
a sob from the woodlot
the rain ruins
houses all the way to the horizon
footsteps are heard
behind a wall without knowing why.

# Équivoque

Équivoque de retrouver belles
des choses
usées et muettes
une pierre est là
dure et veinée
la poésie quelqu'un dit
qu'il n'en veut plus
l'on perçoit l'éclat d'un rire
un sanglot sous les futaies
la pluie détériore
les maisons jusqu'aux horizons
on entend marcher
derrière un mur sans rien savoir.

# In the Morning

Here are the walkers
in small black capes
in worn-out shirts
the floating grasses
the bloody fish
a vendor in rags is selling
in a world captive to students and teachers.
A mirror stays cracked
a door is going to open
a brisk draft of air
can kill you.

## Au matin

Voici les marcheurs
à pèlerines noirâtres
aux blouses qui s'usent
les herbes flottantes
les poissons sanglants
que revend un marchand revêtu de haillons
dans un monde captif d'écoliers et de maîtres.
Une glace reste brisée
une porte va s'ouvrir
un courant d'air vibrant
peut faire mourir.

## Separation

In a shed in the old garden
the separation happens
amidst the rustling of leaves
only far off
in another country
can one recapture this moment of farewell
leaning on the quiet tree
at the lamp hour
when a child is sent
with no confidant
out to fetch milk in the night.

## Séparation

Dans un hangar du vieux jardin
la séparation s'accomplit
aux bruissements des feuillages
il faut s'éloigner
pour un autre pays
pour retrouver ce moment d'adieu
accoté à l'arbre calme
dans l'heure des lampes
alors qu'on envoie un enfant
chercher sans confident
du lait dans la nuit.

## Pretexts

The pretexts for leaving
abound
to hear a footfall again
the sound of a tool
to look once more upon springs, voids
the man sitting never speaking
the tall iron gate of a garden
out of which cries come
surrounded by glass-spiked walls
that loom in the sky
when it storms.

## Prétextes

Pour partir
les prétextes abondent
réentendre un pas
le bruit d'un outil
revoir sources, abîmes
l'homme assis qui ne parle pas
la grille haute d'un jardin
d'où des cris s'élèvent
et qu'entourent des murs à tessons
se dressant sur le ciel
par temps d'orage.

## Town

In a town of tight corners
a clothier stands
on a doorstep
the throne is wobbling
he says looking at the clouds
women, one of them grief-stricken
come to buy despite their failing bodies
a daily loaf
in the shape of a horse collar
and groan at its rising price.

# Bourgade

Dans une bourgade à encoignures
un drapier se tient
sur le pas d'une porte
le trône vacille
déclare-t-il en regardant les nuages
des femmes, dont une en deuil
viennent acheter malgré la déroute de leur corps
un pain coutumier
à forme de collier de cheval
gémissant sur son prix qui monte.

## Beside the Ocean

Reefs bear precious names
the ocean gives in to the moon
the shore fisherman at low tide
comes back carrying green crabs
in a creel of dried willow
as a girl cries out
leave me to my troubles.

## Au bord de mer

Des écueils portent des noms précieux
la mer se soumet à la lune
le pêcheur à pied des marées basses
revient porteur des crabes verts
dans la hotte d'osier mort
lorsqu'une fille s'écrie
laissez-moi à mes peines.

## Not Knowing What Time It Is

Prisoners of war
are all singing
in a no-man's land
not knowing what time it is.
Gardens eked out from the barrens
dug by the light of the moon
meagerly extend
asexual mayflies
churn in the lights
of earthen houses
where tiny lizards feast on them
spread across the dark ceilings.

## Sans connaître l'heure

Prisonniers de guerre
tous chantent
dans un no man's land
sans connaître l'heure.
Des jardins gagnés sur la friche
bêchés au clair de lune
maigrement s'étendent
les éphémères asexués
tourbillonnent autour des lumières
de maisons d'argile
les petits lézards s'en repaissent
étendus sur leurs plafonds noirs.

## Soldier's Words

My forehead my eyes my nose
my mouth speaking to you
do not seem made for this war
the soldier says
the earth is still turning
to the bloodstains of the young
I see foliage tremble
the road bend
the ruin standing tall which no one visits.

## Dire de soldat

Mon front mes yeux mon nez
ma bouche qui vous parle
pour cette guerre ne semblent pas faits
dit le soldat
la terre tourne toujours
aux éclaboussures de jeune sang
je vois trembler le feuillage
s'incurver la route
se dresser la ruine que personne ne visite.

## Under the Sun

A horseman advances
his horse with steaming nostrils
ambles over
the blue ore
leaves wear down beneath a procession of clouds
the waterfall can be heard
in great downrushes
grey rabbits burrow in the fields
under the sun everything appears
a symbol of nothing.

## Sous le soleil

Un cavalier s'avance
son cheval à naseau fumant
va à l'amble
sur le minerai bleu
les feuilles s'usent sous la marche des nuages
on entend la chute d'eau
à grandes retombées
dans les champs fouissent des lapins gris
sous le soleil tout apparaît
symbole de rien.

## Thieves

The ones hiding the stolen reliquary
agree to take it to the peddler and start carrying it
but they always put it back
overhearing it said
you mustn't play with fire
they bang into corners
they hurt themselves
coming and going their dog
cannot suspect a thing
seeing dusk after dusk
sometimes groaning at night.

## Les voleurs

Ceux-là qui cachent le reliquaire volé
conviennent d'aller au receleur le porter
mais remettent toujours
entendent dire
qu'il ne faut pas jouer avec le feu
se cognent aux angles
se font du mal
leur chien allant et venant
ne peut savoir
voit le retour des crépuscules
parfois geint à la nuit.

## Burned Island

From the burned island
one has long remembered
all the shadows of inhabitants
and those of plows and harrows.
There was a loud noise one morning
in all the rooms.
The reality remained
of a child writing so hard on the ruled paper
that on the second line he broke through
bowing the steel pen
while an icy wind picked up
that made the bare branches bend down.

# L'Île brûlée

De l'île brûlée
on s'est longtemps souvenu
de toutes les ombres d'habitants
de celles des herses et charrues.
Il s'y fit un grand bruit certain matin
dans toutes les chambres.
La réalité est restée
d'un enfant écrivant si fortement sur le papier rayé
qu'à la deuxième ligne il le creva
faisant s'infléchir la plume d'acier
alors s'éleva un vent glacé
qui fit se pencher des branches nues.

# The Present

The hems of a garment on a scarecrow
are beating in the earthly wind
a glass-spiked wall is falling in on itself
slim lizards
do not die there
nor the relentless children
throwing stones to the sky
the present flashes
as when it was
devoid of men.

## Le Présent

Les basques d'une vêture d'épouvantail
battent au vent terrien
s'écroule un mur à tessons
les fins lézards
n'en meurent pas
non plus les enfants acharnés
lançant des pierres au ciel
le présent fulgure
comme lorsqu'il était
désert d'hommes.

## Shreddable

The woman looks without speaking
at cloth she thought was durable
shreddable
world she thinks
where nothing lasts
and yet each evening the clinking of tools
can be heard inside the bag
on the back of the man
returning humiliated at the end of the day
while from a lightly-raked path
the smell of food rises.

## Dilacérable

La femme regarde sans voix
l'étoffe qu'elle crut solide
dilacérable
monde pense-t-elle
où rien ne résiste
pourtant on entend chaque soir
au dos le sac
dont s'entrechoquent les outils
celui qui rentre au bout du compte mortifié
tandis que d'une allée
doucement ratissée
monte une odeur de nourriture.

## Deep in the Back

Deep in the back
of the vast attic
where rats feed on poisoned wheat
a ray of sun lights up
the enormous pile of gazettes
out of which comes the musty odor
of a faded century
in the sky soon every light will go out.

# Au fin fond

Au fin fond
dans le grand grenier
où les rats se repaissent de blé empoisonné
un rai de soleil éclaire
le tas énorme des gazettes
d'où monte le remugle
d'un siècle pâli
bientôt au ciel s'éteint toute lumière.

## Something

Called stone eater
a tiny worm consumes the slate
in which it hides
minute by minute time is
tightening its screws
shaken jewelry makes its sound
ants reside in a ruin
something
is always happening.

## Quelque chose

Appelé mangeur de pierre
un petit ver se repaît de l'ardoise
où il se cache
de minute en minute se resserre
l'étau du temps
les bijoux remués font leur bruit
des fourmis habitent une ruine
toujours se passe
quelque chose.

# Edge of the Hearth

The outbuildings with no real use
are left to the rains
a peasant woman
has an edge of the black hearth
for a seat
the evening turns
in swirls of her breath
the wind in the hollow tree
why beings and things
she thinks
and not nothing.

## Bord d'âtre

Les communs sans grand usage
subissent les pluies
une paysanne
a pour s'asseoir
un bord d'âtre noir
dans les remous de son haleine
tourne le soir
dans l'arbre creux le vent
pourquoi êtres et chose sont-ils
plutôt que rien
pense-t-elle.

# Village Square

In the village square
at the foot of the church
one of the drinkers puts on
the kepi of his soldier friend as a joke
above them the hour strikes so loudly
they flinch
a horse that is unhitched
when it stamps the soft earth
radiates an abundant calm
they say to get there
leave before nightfall.

## La Place de commune

Sur une place de commune
au pied de l'église
un des buveurs par jeu
met le képi du compagnon militaire
si fort sonne l'heure au-dessus d'eux
qu'ils en tressaillent
un cheval qu'on dételle
quand il frappe sur la terre meuble
prodigue une douceur fertile
ils disent pour arriver
qu'il faut partir avant la nuit venante.

# Quiet

There is that moment
of hearing water flowing underground
across the clay.
Quiet
the man says to the boy
holding his watch up to his ear
satisfied it ticks so well
in the middle of a tainted century.

## Du calme

Il y a l'instant
que l'on entend l'eau souterraine
coulant à travers l'argile.
Du calme
dit l'homme à l'enfant
lui mettant la montre à l'oreille
content qu'elle batte si bien
au milieu du siècle impur.

# A Night

Organ function is breaking down
the hand stays pressed
to the craggy wall
then the body with neither hearth nor home
continues on through a cold night
and starts forging words
to speak in the coming daylight.

# Une nuit

Le travail des organes s'épuise
la main au mur grumeleux
reste appuyée
puis le corps sans feu ni lieu
s'avance dans une nuit froide
et se met à forger des mots
à dire au jour venu.

## Moment of a World

In the smoky town
with blows of their sabers
soldiers are killing geese
hardwood trees
grow in force on the square
the future will have the same gleams
but no longer
resting on the table
the gloved hand
of a loner
who hardly ever speaks.

## Moment d'un monde

Au bourg à fumées
des soldats à coups de sabre tuent des oies
sur la place montent en force
les arbres durs
mêmes lueurs dans l'avenir
mais plus la main gantée
sur la table posée
d'un solitaire
qui ne parle presque jamais.

## A Ring of Keys

Senseless dreams
wear out the man waking
in his iron bed
painted the color of bronze
he is amazed at life
and at each object
seen in reality
or in the mirror that reflected
for just one morning
the face of a woman
marked by age
but every day a ring of keys
one of them spotted with rust.

## Un trousseau de clefs

Des rêves à non sens
épuisent l'homme au réveil
dans son lit de fer
peint couleur de bronze
il s'étonne de vivre
et de chaque objet
vu en réel
ou dans la glace qui ne refléta
qu'un matin
un visage de femme
que marquait l'âge
mais chaque jour un trousseau de clefs
dont l'une s'est marquée de rouille.

# Acknowledgments

I am grateful to the editors of the journals in which the following translations appeared, sometimes in earlier versions:

*Tupelo Quarterly*: Masons of 1830, History, Artisans, In Humans, Dogs, The Plant, Earthly Things, Shreddable, Village Square

*Laurel Review*: The Fire, The Shop, The Corncrake, Black Rain, Something, Moment of a World

Thank you, Carey McHugh and Robert Ostrom, for your many helpful comments on the manuscript.

Thank you, Ben Estes and Alan Felsenthal, for bringing Jean Follain to The Song Cave.

And thank you, Sofia, for listening to these poems over the last few years.

# Bibliography


## Poetry

*La Main chaude* (1933)
*Chants terrestres* (1937)
*Ici-bas* (1941)
*Transparence du monde* (1942-1943)
*Usage de temps* (collection of his first four volumes; 1943)
*Exister* (1947)
*Territoires* (1953)
*Tout instant* (1957)
*Des heures* (1960)
*Poèmes et proses choisis (1961)*
*Appareil de la terre* (1964)
*D'Après tout* (1967)
*Espaces d'instants* (1971)

## Prose

*Paris* (1935)
*L'Épicerie d'enfance* (1938)
*Canisy* (1942)
*Chef-lieu* (1950)
*Célébration de la pomme de terre* (1966)
*Collège* (1973)

## Other

*Saint Jean-Marie Vianney, Curé d'Ars* (1959)
*Pérou* (1964)
*Petit glossaire de l'argot ecclésiastique* (1966)

## OTHER TITLES FROM THE SONG CAVE:

1. *A Dark Dreambox of Another Kind* by **Alfred Starr Hamilton**
2. *My Enemies* by **Jane Gregory**
3. *Rude Woods* by **Nate Klug**
4. *Georges Braque and Others* by **Trevor Winkfield**
5. *The Living Method* by **Sara Nicholson**
6. *Splash State* by **Todd Colby**
7. *Essay Stanzas* by **Thomas Meyer**
8. *Illustrated Games of Patience* by **Ben Estes**
9. *Dark Green* by **Emily Hunt**
10. *Honest James* by **Christian Schlegel**
11. *M* by **Hannah Brooks-Motl**
12. *What the Lyric Is* by **Sara Nicholson**
13. *The Hermit* by **Lucy Ives**
14. *The Orchid Stories* by **Kenward Elmslie**
15. *Do Not Be a Gentleman When You Say Goodnight* by **Mitch Sisskind**
16. *HAIRDO* by **Rachel B. Glaser**
17. *Motor Maids across the Continent* by **Ron Padgett**
18. *Songs for Schizoid Siblings* by **Lionel Ziprin**
19. *Professionals of Hope: The Selected Writings of* **Subcomandante Marcos**
20. *Fort Not* by **Emily Skillings**
21. *Riddles, Etc.* by **Geoffrey Hilsabeck**
22. *CHARAS: The Improbable Dome Builders* by **Syeus Mottel** (Co-published with Pioneer Works)
23. *YEAH NO* by **Jane Gregory**

24. *Nioque of the Early-Spring* by **Francis Ponge**
25. *Smudgy and Lossy* by **John Myers**
26. *The Desert* by **Brandon Shimoda**
27. *Scardanelli* by **Friederike Mayröcker**
28. *The Alley of Fireflies and Other Stories* by **Raymond Roussel**
29. *CHANGES: Notes on Choreography* by **Merce Cunningham** (Co-published with the Merce Cunningham Trust)
30. *My Mother Laughs* by **Chantal Akerman**
31. *Earth* by **Hannah Brooks-Motl**
32. *Everything and Other Poems* by **Charles North**
33. *Paper Bells* by **Phan Nhiên Hạo**
34. *Photographs: Together & Alone* by **Karlheinz Weinberger**
35. *A Better Place Is Hard to Find* by **Aaron Fagan**
36. *Rough Song* by **Blanca Varela**
37. *In the Same Light: 200 Poems for Our Century From the Migrants & Exiles of the Tang Dynasty,* translated by **Wong May**
38. *On the Mesa: An Anthology of Bolinas Writing (50th Anniversary Edition),* edited by **Ben Estes and Joel Weishaus**
39. *Listen My Friend, This Is the Dream I Dreamed Last Night* by **Cody-Rose Clevidence**
40. *Poetries* by **Georges Schehadé**
41. *Wings in Time* by **Callie Garnett**
42. *Two Murals* by **Jesús Castillo**
43. *Punks: New & Selected Poems* by **John Keene**
44. *ABC Moonlight* by **Ben Estes**
45. *Star Lake* by **Arda Collins**
46. *The Maybe-Bird* by **Jennifer Elise Foerster**
47. *Seriously Well* by **Helge Torvund**

48. *Dereliction* by **Gabrielle Octavia Rucker**

49. *Bookworm: Conversations with* **Michael Silverblatt**

50. *April* by **Sara Nicholson**

51. *Valley of the Many-Colored Grasses* by **Ronald Johnson**

52. *The Sphinx and the Milky Way: Selections from the Notebooks of* **Charles Burchfield**

53. *Telling the Truth as It Comes Up: Selected Talks & Essays 1991–2018* by **Alice Notley**

54. *Lunar Solo: Selected Poems* by **Jules Laforgue**

55. *Stranger* by **Emily Hunt**

56. *The Selkie* by **Morgan Võ**

57. *Hereafter* by **Alan Felsenthal**

58. *Cold Dogs* by **Zan de Parry**

59. *Saturday* by **Margaret Ross**

60. *Many Poems* by **Roberta Iannamico**

61. *Ultraviolet of the Genuine* by **Hannah Brooks-Motl**

62. *Silkworm's Pansori* by **David Seung**

63. *Tantrums in Air* by **Emily Skillings**

64. *Jump Cuts: Essays on Surrealism, Film, Music, Culture, and Other Utopian Topics* by **Mark Polizzotti**